MORLEY LIBRARY

3 0112 1060 4578 1

Y0-CJG-909

CHARACTER EDUCATION

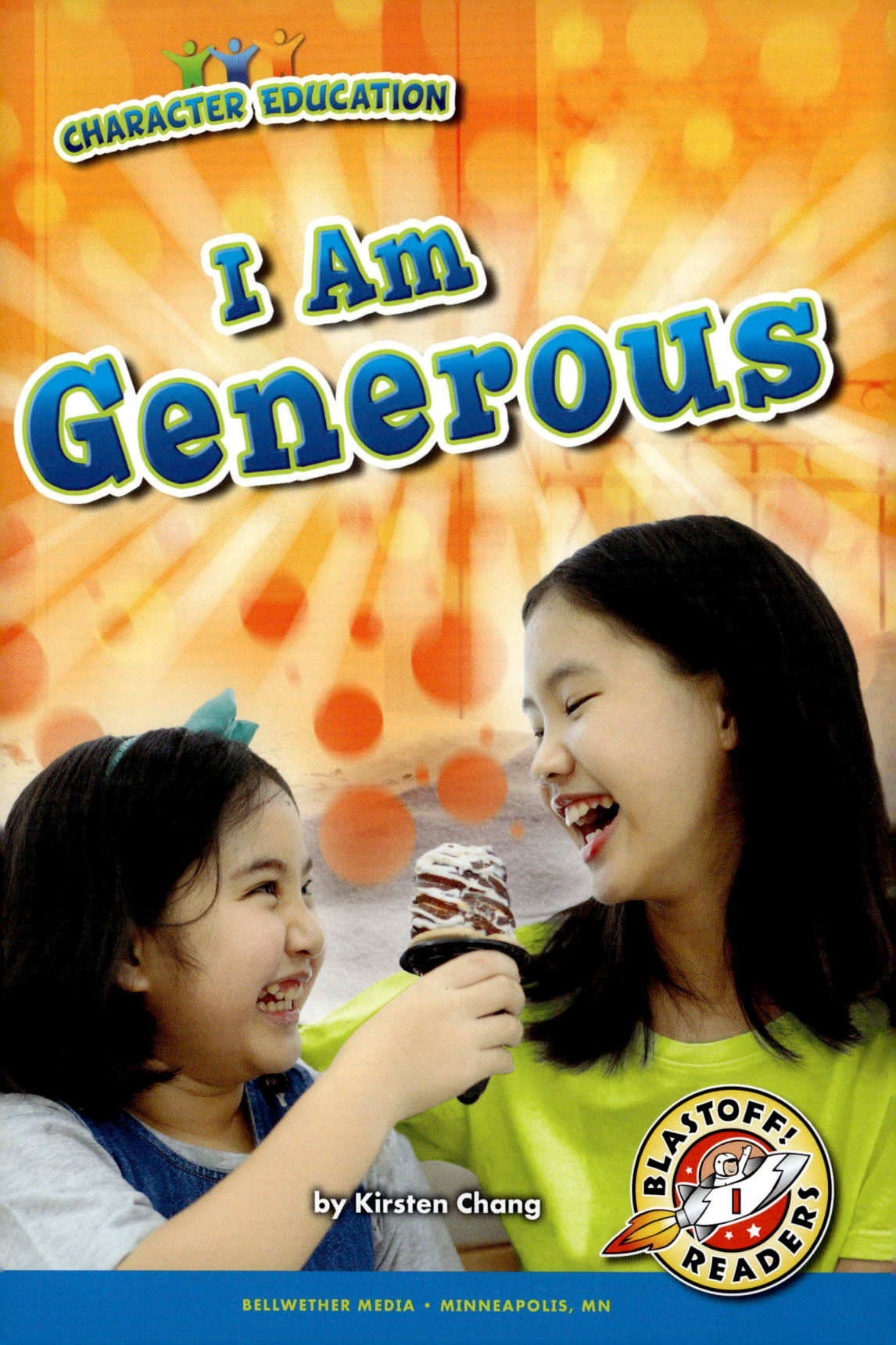

I Am Generous

by Kirsten Chang

BLASTOFF! READERS

BELLWETHER MEDIA • MINNEAPOLIS, MN

Note to Librarians, Teachers, and Parents:

Blastoff! Readers are carefully developed by literacy experts and combine standards-based content with developmentally appropriate text.

Level 1 provides the most support through repetition of high-frequency words, light text, predictable sentence patterns, and strong visual support.

Level 2 offers early readers a bit more challenge through varied simple sentences, increased text load, and less repetition of high-frequency words.

Level 3 advances early-fluent readers toward fluency through increased text and concept load, less reliance on visuals, longer sentences, and more literary language.

Level 4 builds reading stamina by providing more text per page, increased use of punctuation, greater variation in sentence patterns, and increasingly challenging vocabulary.

Level 5 encourages children to move from "learning to read" to "reading to learn" by providing even more text, varied writing styles, and less familiar topics.

Whichever book is right for your reader, Blastoff! Readers are the perfect books to build confidence and encourage a love of reading that will last a lifetime!

This edition first published in 2020 by Bellwether Media, Inc.

No part of this publication may be reproduced in whole or in part without written permission of the publisher. For information regarding permission, write to Bellwether Media, Inc., Attention: Permissions Department, 6012 Blue Circle Drive, Minnetonka, MN 55343.

Library of Congress Cataloging-in-Publication Data

Names: Chang, Kirsten, 1991- author.
Title: I Am Generous / by Kirsten Chang.
Description: Minneapolis : Bellwether Media, 2020. | Series: Character education |
  Includes bibliographical references and index. | Audience: Ages 5-8 | Audience: Grades K-1 |
  Summary: "Developed by literacy experts for students in kindergarten through grade three, this book
  introduces generosity to young readers through leveled text and related photos"--Provided by publisher.
Identifiers: LCCN 2019024640 (print) | LCCN 2019024641 (ebook) | ISBN 9781644871119 (library binding) |
  ISBN 9781618917911 (paperback) | ISBN 9781618917812 (ebook)
Subjects: LCSH: Generosity--Juvenile literature. | Values--Juvenile literature.
Classification: LCC BJ1533.G4 C42 2020 (print) | LCC BJ1533.G4 (ebook) | DDC 179/.9--dc23
LC record available at https://lccn.loc.gov/2019024640
LC ebook record available at https://lccn.loc.gov/2019024641

Text copyright © 2020 by Bellwether Media, Inc. BLASTOFF! READERS and associated logos are trademarks and/or registered trademarks of Bellwether Media, Inc.

Editor: Christina Leaf   Designer: Jeffrey Kollock

Printed in the United States of America, North Mankato, MN.

Table of Contents

What Is Generosity? 4
Why Be Generous? 10
You Are Generous! 16
Glossary 22
To Learn More 23
Index 24

What Is Generosity?

Your friend wants to play with your favorite toy.

5

Do you keep it
for yourself?
Or are you generous?

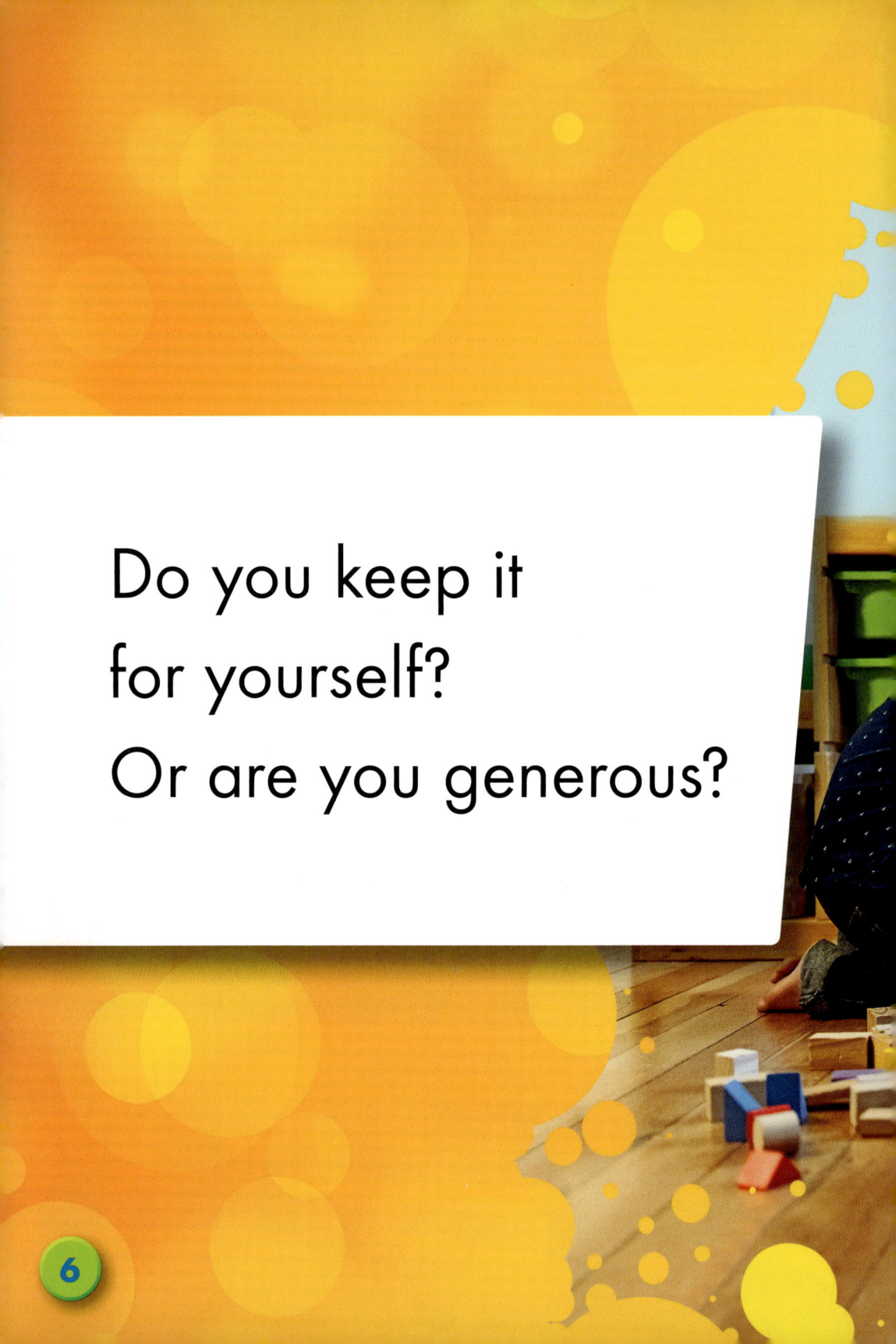

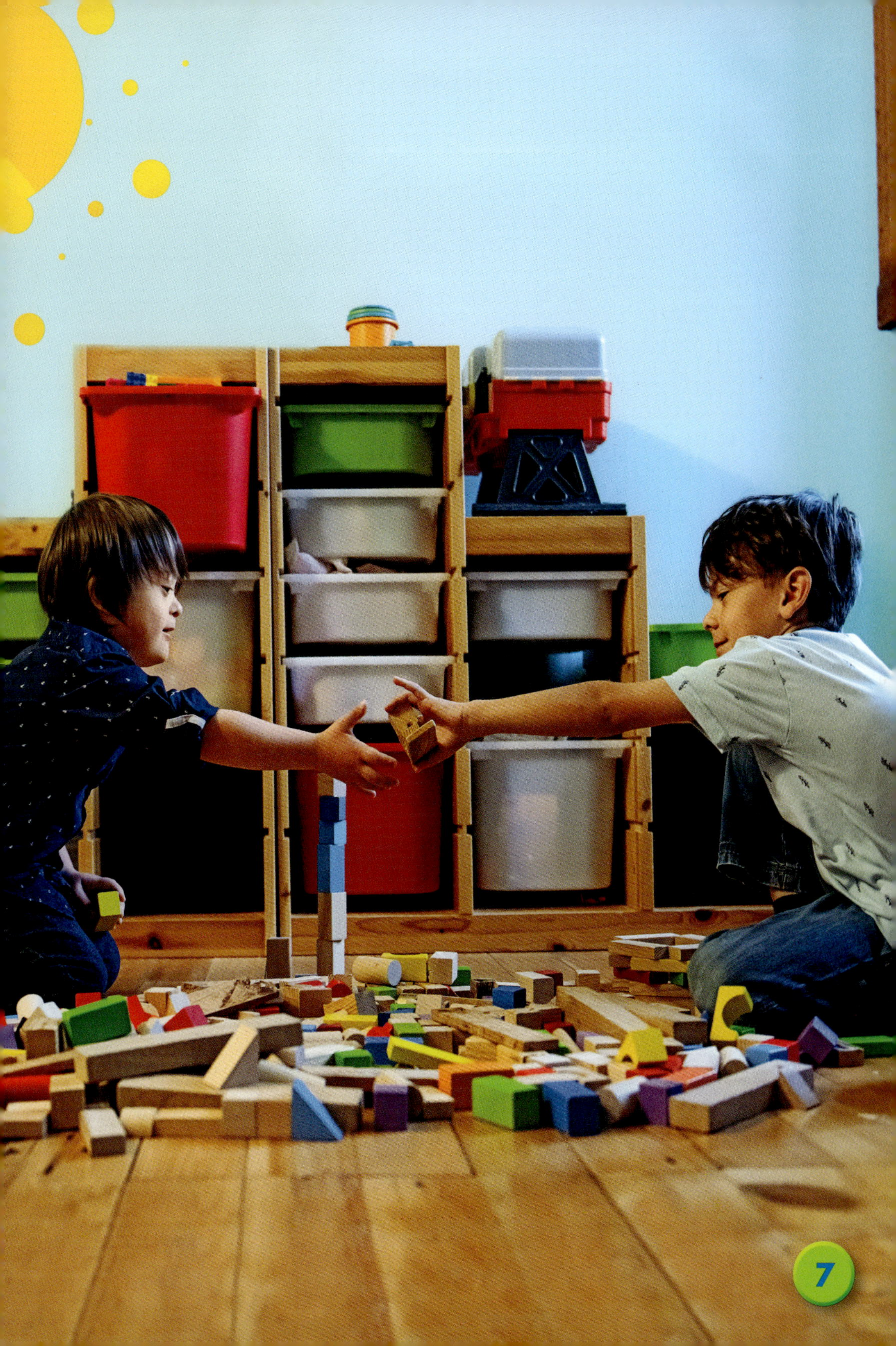

Generous people **share** with others. They give time, money, or things.

9

Why Be Generous?

Generosity builds **relationships**. It makes people happy. You feel happy, too!

11

Others may feel hurt if you are **selfish**.

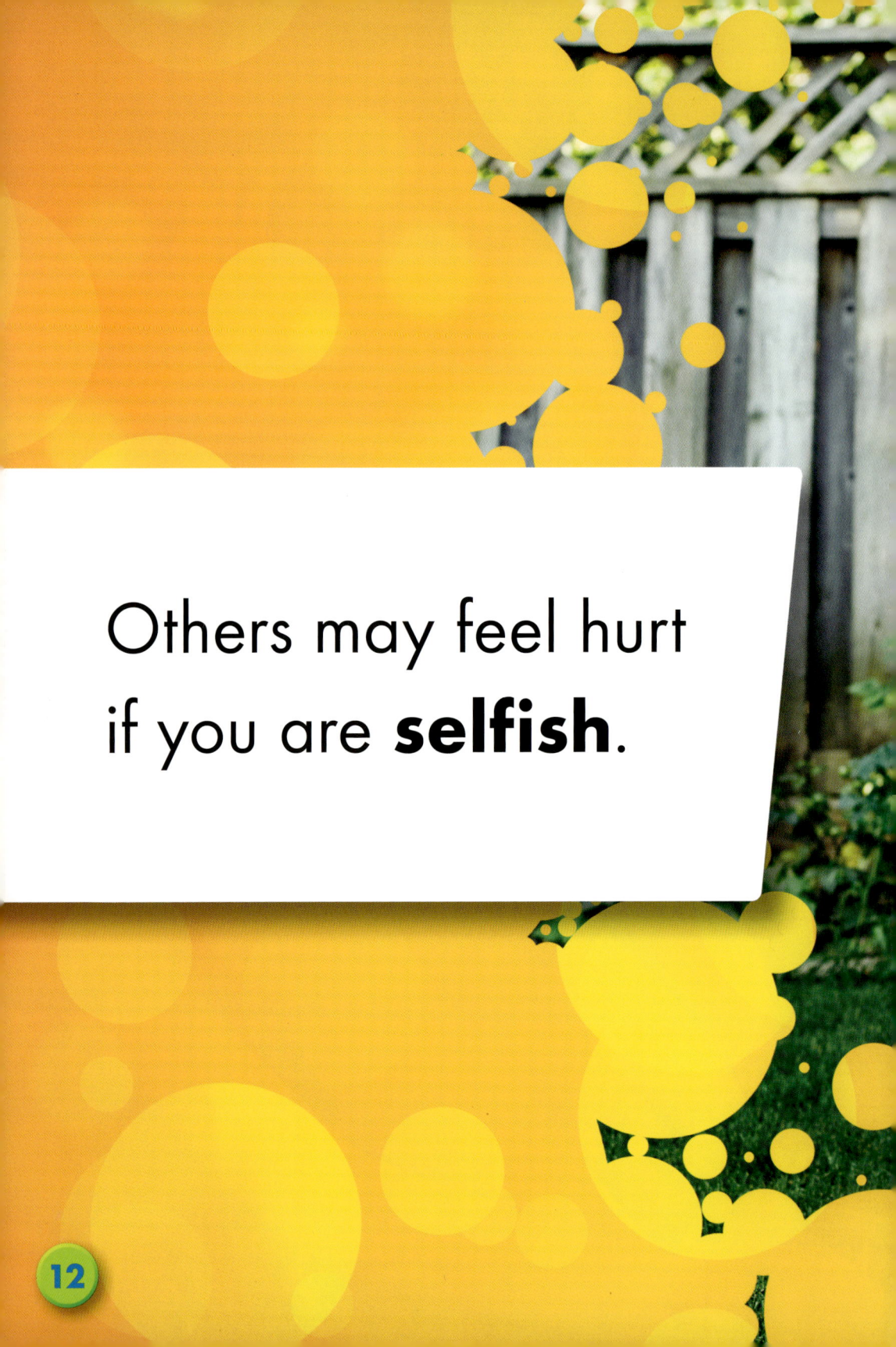

13

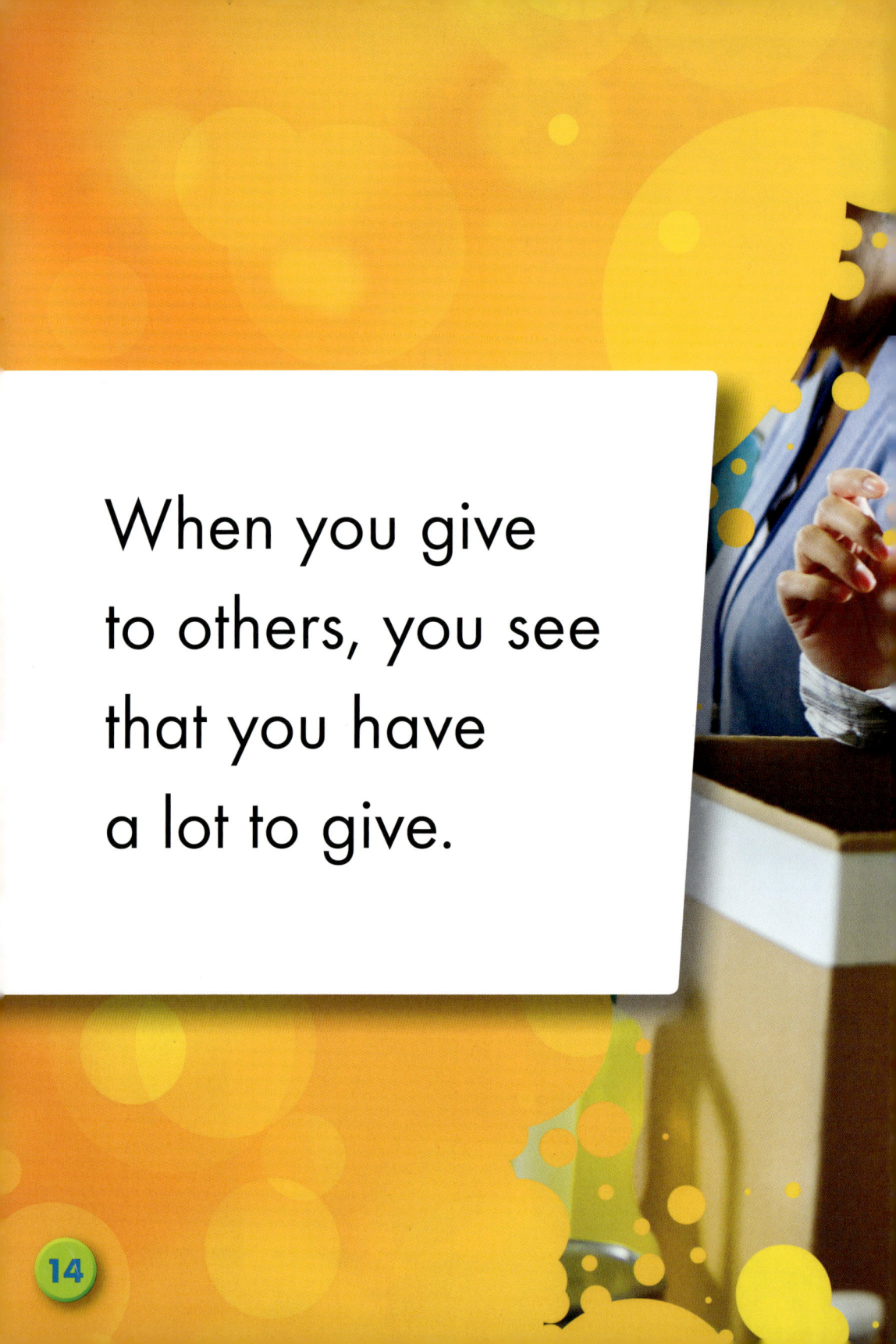

When you give to others, you see that you have a lot to give.

Who Is Generous?

15

You Are Generous!

You can be generous! Ellie **donates** her hair to help kids who are sick.

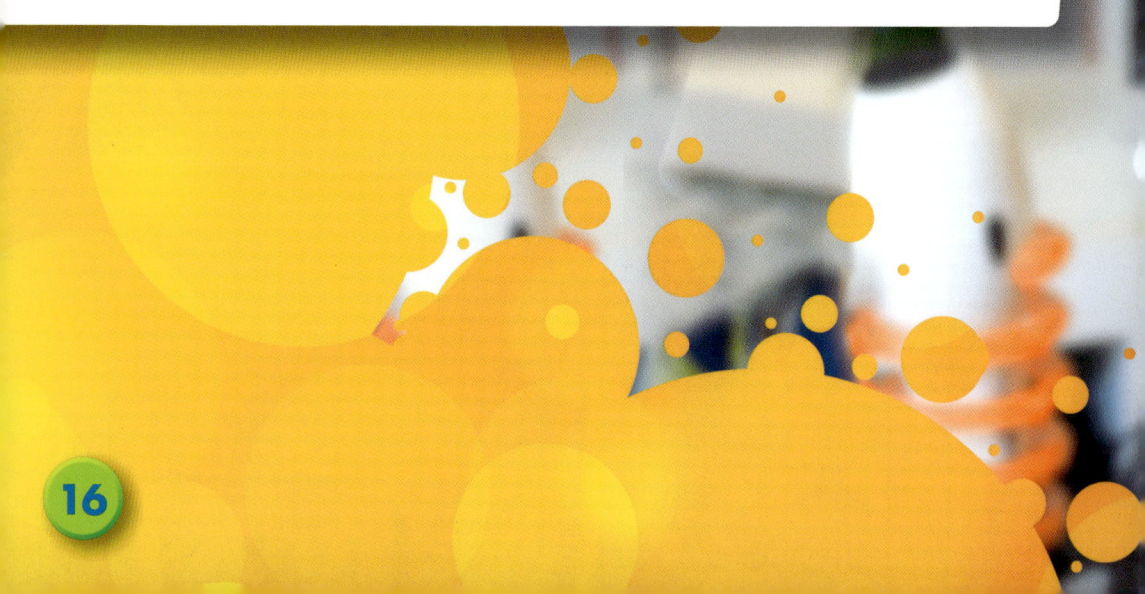

17

Alicia shares her time. She helps her parents with a **chore**.

19

Nick raises money for a good **cause**. How are you generous?

21

Glossary

cause
something people believe in and want to help

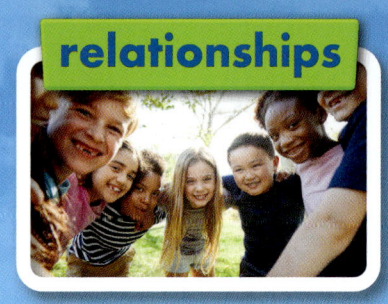

relationships
ties between people

chore
a duty

selfish
thinking only of oneself

donates
gives something to a person or a group to help them

share
to let someone have or use something that belongs to you

To Learn More

AT THE LIBRARY

DiOrio, Rana. *What Does It Mean to Be Kind?* San Francisco, Calif.: Little Pickle Press, 2015.

Pettiford, Rebecca. *Showing Generosity.* Minneapolis, Minn.: Bullfrog Books, 2018.

Shepherd, Jodie. *Kindness and Generosity: It Starts with Me.* New York, N.Y.: Children's Press, 2016.

ON THE WEB

FACTSURFER

Factsurfer.com gives you a safe, fun way to find more information.

1. Go to www.factsurfer.com.

2. Enter "generous" into the search box and click 🔍.

3. Select your book cover to see a list of related web sites.

Index

cause, 20
chore, 18
donates, 16
feel, 10, 12
friend, 4
give, 8, 14
hair, 16
help, 16, 18
money, 8, 20
parents, 18
play, 4
relationships, 10
selfish, 12
share, 8, 18
things, 8

time, 8, 18
toy, 4
Who Is?, 15

The images in this book are reproduced through the courtesy of: Ronnachai Palas, front cover; lisegagne, pp. 4-5, 6-7; szefei, pp. 8-9; Robert Kneschke, pp. 10-11; Anna Kraynova, pp. 12-13; asiseeit, pp. 14-15; MajaArgakijeva, p. 15 (bottom left, bottom right); MaeManee, pp. 16-17; Odua Images, pp. 18-19; New Africa, pp. 20-21; Monkey Business Images, p. 22 (cause, relationships); Rawpixel.com, p. 22 (chore); Makistock, p. 22 (donates); Zabavna, p. 22 (selfish); DenisProduction.com, p. 22 (share).